Children of the World

Peru

For a free color catalog describing Gareth Stevens' list of high-quality books, call 1-800-341-3569 (USA) or 1-800-461-9120 (Canada).

For their help in the preparation of *Children of the World: Peru,* the authors and editor gratefully acknowledge the help of Assistant US Secretary of State Betty Tamposi, US Consul General Wayne Griffith, Norma Cobacha, James Blanford of the US State Department Bureau of Consular Affairs, Frank Sibley, American Airlines, which generously provided transporation, and Dora Diaz of Mount Mary College, Milwaukee, Wisconsin.

Flag illustration on page 48, © Flag Research Center.

Library of Congress Cataloging-in-Publication Data

Rogers, Barbara Radcliffe.
    Peru / written by Barbara Radcliffe Rogers : Photography by Stillman Rogers.
      p. cm. -- (Children of the world)
    Includes index.
    Summary: Presents the life of a twelve-year-old girl in Lima, Peru, describing her home and school activities and discussing the history, geography, ethnic composition, culture, and other aspects of her country.
    ISBN 0-8368-0235-7
    1. Peru--Social life and customs. 2. Children--Peru. [1. Peru--Social life and customs. 2. Family life--Peru.] I. Rogers, Stillman. 1939- ill. II. Series: Children of the world (Milwaukee, Wis.)
    F3410.R57 1992   89-43183
    985—dc20

Edited, designed, and produced by
Gareth Stevens Publishing
1555 North RiverCenter Drive, Suite 201
Milwaukee, Wisconsin 53212, USA

Series editor: Valerie Weber
Research editor: Chandrika Kaul, Ph.D.
Designer: Beth Karpfinger
Map design: Sheri Gibbs

Printed in the United States of America

1 2 3 4 5 6 7 8 9 98 97 96 95 94 93 92

Children of the World
Peru

Text by Barbara Radcliffe Rogers
Photographs by Stillman Rogers

Gareth Stevens Publishing
MILWAUKEE

. . . a note about *Children of the World:*

The children of the world live in fishing towns, Arctic regions, and urban centers, on islands and in mountain valleys, on sheep ranches and fruit farms. This series follows one child in each country through the pattern of his or her life. Candid photographs show the children with their families, at school, at play, and in their communities. The text describes the dreams of the children and, often through their own words, tells how they see themselves and their lives.

Each book also explores events that are unique to the country in which the child lives, including festivals, religious ceremonies, and national holidays. The *Children of the World* series does more than tell about foreign countries. It introduces the children of each country and shows readers what it is like to be a child in that country.

Children of the World includes the following published and to-be-published titles:

Afghanistan	El Salvador	Jordan	Saudi Arabia
Argentina	England	Kenya	Singapore
Australia	Finland	Malaysia	South Africa
Austria	France	Mexico	South Korea
Belize	Greece	Morocco	Spain
Bhutan	Guatemala	Nepal	Sweden
Bolivia	Honduras	New Zealand	Tanzania
Brazil	Hong Kong	Nicaragua	Thailand
Burma (Myanmar)	Hungary	Nigeria	Turkey
Canada	India	Norway	USSR
China	Indonesia	Panama	Vietnam
Costa Rica	Ireland	Peru	West Germany
Cuba	Israel	Philippines	Yugoslavia
Czechoslovakia	Italy	Poland	Zambia
Denmark	Jamaica	Portugal	
Egypt	Japan	Romania	

. . . and about *Peru:*

Twelve-year-old Anna Patricia Martinez, known as Patita, lives with her large extended family in Lima, Peru's seaside capital. Although her father is dead, the men in her extended family act as surrogate fathers, and her best friends are her family. While attending one of the best schools in Lima, Patita learns fascinating details about her country's colorful past and, aided by her brother, becomes proficient on the computer.

To enhance this book's value in libraries and classrooms, comprehensive reference sections include up-to-date information about Peru's geography, demographics, languages, currency, education, cultures, industry, and natural resources. *Peru* also features a bibliography, glossaries, activities and research projects, and discussions of such subjects as Lima, the country's history, languages, political system, and ethnic and religious composition.

The living conditions and experiences of children in Peru vary according to economic, environmental, and ethnic circumstances. The reference sections help bring to life for young readers the diversity and richness of the culture and heritage of Peru. Of particular interest are discussions of the powerful Inca empire that once ruled all of Peru and much of South America and the country's current economic and political woes.

CONTENTS

LIVING IN PERU:
Anna Patricia, a Serious Student

Anna Patricia Martinez is a 12-year-old girl from Peru, a country on the west coast of South America. Her home is in Jesús María, a section of Peru's capital city of Lima.

Anna Patricia lives with her mother, Anna Losada de Martinez; her brother, Enrique, who is 25; and her mother's parents. Because her mother's name is also Anna, her family calls her Patita, which is the way to say "Patty" in Spanish.

Her whole name is Anna Patricia Martinez Losada, which shows that her father's last name was Martinez and her mother's Losada. But like most people in Peru, she hardly ever uses the last name.

Patita gives a warm "Hello." *"Buenas dias!* My name is Anna Patricia Martinez. This is my mother." ▶

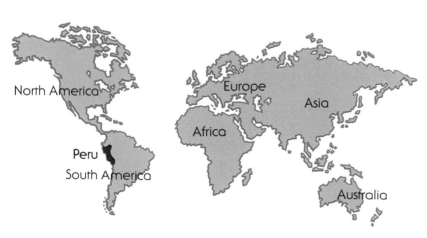

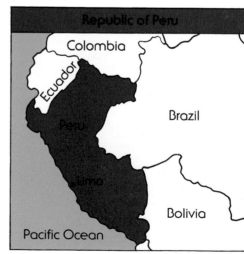

Lima has many public parks and squares with benches so people can sit and enjoy the gardens and shade trees.

Living in Lima

Lima is not only a very big city but also a very old one. Many of its buildings, especially the churches, were built over 400 years ago in an ornate Spanish style. These, along with Lima's wide streets and large squares with fountains and trees, give the city an elegant, graceful look.

Patita's neighborhood is one of Lima's newer ones. The streets are wide, and the homes are built of brick covered with stucco. Almost all of the houses have tiny front yards filled with huge flowering bushes and shrubs. Plants such as poinsettias and geraniums grow to be taller than people.

Patita's neighborhood is not a wealthy one, but it is neater and cleaner than some other neighborhoods in Lima. Many Indian families who have moved from the Andes Mountains to the city have no place to live and no jobs. So they have built houses on empty lots, using whatever materials they can find. Without electricity or running water, these *pueblos jovenes*, or young villages, are crowded and dirty. They are much poorer than Jesús María.

The oldest part of Lima is in its center. Outlying neighborhoods grew around little villages and soon became part of the city itself. In the centers of these newer neighborhoods are often fine old churches that once stood in the center of the village.

Top: Many of the homes in Patita's neighborhood have several apartments belonging to different generations of the same family.

Bottom: Indians who have moved into Lima from the mountains often sell food, cooking it right on the street.

The Family Sticks Together

When Patita was six years old, her father became ill with cancer and died. Without the income from his job with an oil company, Patita's family could not afford to live in a house of their own. So they moved into Patita's grandparents' home.

It is not at all unusual in Peru for several generations of a family to live together in the same house. Grown sons and daughters are expected to live with their parents until they get married.

In the house next door live Patita's aunt and uncle and their two grown daughters. When another aunt and uncle could not afford the high cost of owning a home, Patita's grandparents helped them build a third-story addition onto the house next door. They live there with their three children — Carla, Augusto, and Enrique.

Patita's Uncle Pedro, who lives neaby, comes to her house often. He thinks she is far too serious all the time and tells jokes to make her laugh. He enjoys sports and encourages Patita to play basketball and volleyball. For her birthday last December, he bought her a bicycle.

Patita's aunts and cousins all feel right at home in her grandparents' house.

Because Patita was so young when her father died, all the men in the family are careful to make sure she has someone to be like a father to her now. She is especially close to her grandfather. When she finishes her homework in the evening, she will often curl up on the rug by his chair, where they will talk or watch TV. Sometimes her cousins from next door will join them there.

The homes of all of Patita's relatives are like a small neighborhood. Even though each apartment has a separate entrance, they all connect in the backyard. Yards like these, with tall walls around them, are very common in South America. They are like an extra room, a place to hang laundry and for children to play.

The grandparents' house is home to everyone — aunts, cousins, and uncles — all stop by to visit or share a pie they've baked or join in a meal. Holidays such as Christmas are celebrated with a festive dinner at the big table with all 15 cousins and their parents.

◀ The Losada family has added rooms on top of their home to make more living space.

Patita's favorite place in the evening is next to her grandfather's chair.

Family and Friends — One and the Same

Patita's older brother is named Enrique, a common name in the Losada family. Enrique is mildly mentally retarded. Peru has no special schools for students with special needs, but his family and teachers have helped and encouraged him to complete a regular high school education.

Although many skills are difficult for Enrique to learn, he is very good at using a computer. He also enjoys teaching Patita how to work with it. Enrique feels good that he is able to teach his little sister something that will help her in school.

Enrique's family bought him a computer of his own, which he uses to type papers for university students and for other temporary jobs.

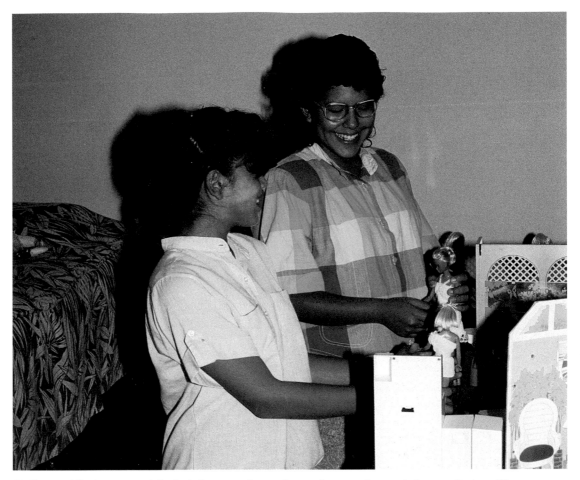

Carlita and Patita pretend their dolls are going to fancy dress parties and change their outfits.

Patita also often spends time with her best friend and cousin, Carla — or Carlita, as everyone in the family calls her. She just turned 13 and is a year ahead of Patita in school. Because the cousins live next to each other, they can play together whenever they want.

Their favorite pastime is playing with their Barbie dolls. They dress them up for sports and special occasions and pretend they live in the pink doll house in Patita's bedroom. The time goes by so quickly that they are surprised when their grandmother calls them downstairs to set the table for dinner.

A Rush to School

On school days, Patita wakes up before 7:00 a.m., makes her bed, combs her hair, and eats a quick breakfast. Then she puts on her school uniform — a gray jumper with a white blouse under it. The skirt is too long, she grumbles, and gray is such a dull color. She would much rather go to school in a bright, comfortable T-shirt and a pair of cut-off jeans.

"Hurry, Carlita!" she calls up the stairs as she packs her books and notebooks into her bag. But there is still no sign of her cousin. So Patita runs upstairs to hurry her along. School is a 20-minute walk from their house, but if they are late, their grandfather will drive them.

School begins at 8:00 a.m. Patita goes directly to her locker and puts on a yellow smock over her school uniform. Each class has a different color smock (Carlita's is blue), and they wear that color from seventh through eleventh grade, when they graduate.

Top: At least the smocks come in brighter colors than the uniforms!
Bottom: The Maria Alvarado School was built in 1906.

18

You can tell the students' classes by the colors of their smocks.

Anna Patricia's class.

Maria Alvarado School — A Family Tradition

The Maria Alvarado School was begun in 1906 by Methodist missionaries from the United States because there were no good schools for girls at the time. Now that girls have an equal chance in the public schools, the school has less reason to be exclusively for girls and admits boys. Patita's mother and all but two of her cousins attended this same school, so it is now a family tradition to go there.

Most of the students are Catholic, as is Patita, but they all study religion and attend a Methodist church service once each week. Every school day begins with a prayer.

The school building is big, with three separate courtyards inside. One looks like a park, with a smooth green lawn, shrubs, and bright flowers. The hallways on each floor open out onto these courtyards, which helps keep the school bright, cool, and cheerful.

The classrooms are large, but Patita's seventh grade class is so big this year, it had to be divided in half. There are six years of elementary school and five years of high school — from grades seven through eleven.

Left: The art classes set their easels in the open corridor for the best light.

Below: In most classes, there are now equal numbers of girls and boys.

All students take the same subjects, so instead of having students change rooms between class periods, the teachers move. The first class of the morning is natural science, then math, Spanish language and literature, social studies, and English, Patita's favorite.

After fifth period, everyone goes out into the huge back courtyard for lunch. Patita meets Carla there, and sometimes they eat together. Other days, Patita eats with a group of girls from her own class. Most of the students bring their lunches from home and buy drinks from a counter in the school yard. Patita and Carla have vegetables and fruit for lunch.

Each day's classes are different in the afternoons. One day, they have physical education for two class periods in a row. They spend two months learning each sport. Other days, they have music, gardening, or patriotism class, which teaches about Peru's heroes. On Thursdays, they have a painting class in the courtyard, and Patita stays after school that day for painting club.

Her teacher watches as Patita writes a sentence on the blackboard.

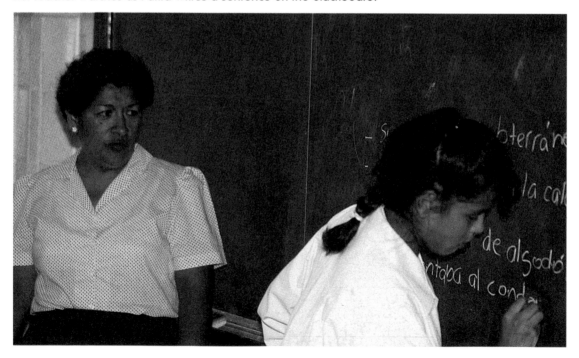

The girls sit in circles in the school yard to eat their lunch.

Students can buy drinks from a snack bar right in the school yard.

Because Lima's climate is so mild, flowers bloom all year round and grow to be quite large.

Top: Her teacher is pleased that Patita has a chance to practice on a computer at home as well as at school.

Bottom: Typing is a required course for all students.

The Maria Alvarado School is one of the most advanced in Peru. Each student must learn to use a computer as well as a typewriter before graduation.

The director of the school is very proud of the record of Maria Alvarado's graduates as they move into their careers. Only about 10% of all Peruvians graduating from high school qualify for admission to universities, but over 90% of Maria Alvarado's graduates are accepted! All of the school's graduates go on to advanced schooling of some kind.

Patita's family does not have to pay any tuition to send her to private school. Because she was already a student there when her father died, the school gave her a scholarship.

She is a very serious student and always finishes her work, so all her teachers expect that she will be accepted at a university. She will be able to choose from a variety of careers that interest her, since women in Peru have greater opportunities than ever before.

In addition to the usual subjects, Maria Alvarado School has begun to teach gardening this year. One of the small courtyards has been divided into neat, raised garden beds where students are learning to grow fruit, vegetables, and herbs. The climate of Lima is warm all year round, but it hardly ever rains. The students will have to be careful that the ground does not dry out, or they will never harvest any crops.

There are no study hall periods at school, so when Patita needs to use the library, she does it during her lunch hour. The library is a large, bright place to study.

Left: The gardening project teaches students how they can grow food in small backyard gardens at home.

Below: Patita checks out books from the school library whenever she has a report to write.

People of the early civilizations of Peru often made their pottery in the shapes of fanciful animals and birds.

Learning about Peru's History

In the library is a small museum, where Patita and her friends like to look at pottery made in Peru over 1,000 years ago. The pottery is especially interesting to them this year because they are studying Peru's history in social studies class.

Anna Patricia has never had a chance to visit Cuzco, the mountain city where the Inca rulers had their capital 500 years ago. Some day, she would like to see the famous Temple of the Sun, where an entire garden of gold and silver corn and other plants once stood before the Spanish conquered the Incas and sent all the gold to Spain.

Today, this area is still more Indian than Spanish. Most women still wear their traditional full skirts and felt hats. Inca holidays such as *Inti Raymi,* the Feast of the Sun, are celebrated along with Catholic holidays. On the terraced mountainsides, Indians still raise corn and potatoes using foot plows and short hand hoes, the same methods used for farming when the Incas ruled the land.

Left, top: This woman is weaving a complicated design like the one in the shawl she is wearing.

Left, bottom: Women can spin as they walk, even on rough, uneven trails.

In the high Andes Mountains that surround Cuzco stand the ruins of several Inca cities. The best known is Machu Picchu, which was a religious center perched on a steep mountain.

Although the Incas did not use either wheels or animals to move stones up the steep mountainsides, they built walls of stones weighing several tons each. Their stonecutters were so expert that even today a knife blade cannot be slipped between the stones they fitted together.

For Patita, visiting Macchu Picchu and Cuzco would seem like stepping five centuries back into the history of her country. She would be able to walk along streets between Inca walls and even pick up pieces of their pottery in the deserted towns.

In the mountain villages near Cuzco, she could see herds of llamas and watch women spinning their wool into yarn on hand spindles. She could see other women in front of their small farmhouses weaving brightly colored *llicllas* (YEEK-yahs), the shawls in which they carry babies on their backs. Life in these mountain villages is much different from life in Patita's Lima neighborhood.

Thatch made of grass or leaves is a common roofing material in the mountain villages near Cuzco.

30

Both llamas and alpacas provide warm wool for clothing and blankets.

Inset: This Indian woman is separating wool fibers so she can spin the wool into yarn. Her drop spindle is in front of her.

Only the walls remain of the ancient buildings in Machu Picchu, an Inca city high in the Andes.

After School

The first thing Patita does when she gets home from school at 3:30 p.m. is have something to eat. She is so hungry that she doesn't even change out of her school uniform first! Today she is very lucky — her grandmother saved her a piece of the delicious *Pastelle de Manzanas* that her Aunt Mercedes brought for Sunday dinner. This is like apple pie, but the crust is sweeter, almost like a sugar cookie.

"I don't have a lot of studying tonight," Carlita calls from the stairway in the backyard. The girls agree to meet there as soon as Patita's homework is finished.

But most evenings, Patita has no time to play with her cousin. She usually studies from 4:30 to 9:00 p.m., with time out only to eat dinner with her family. Sometimes she even brings a book downstairs to the backyard to study between her dinnertime chores.

After she has helped wash and chop vegetables, Patita studies on the patio next to the kitchen until dinnertime. ▶

Patita studies English and the history of the Incas, who once ruled Peru and much of South America.

But First, an Errand

Before Patita begins her homework, she changes from her school uniform into comfortable blue jeans and a T-shirt and goes to the bakery to buy bread for dinner. Sometimes she walks to the bakery, which is only three blocks from her house, and other days she rides her bicycle.

The bakery is quite small and also carries cheese, drinks, and a few other groceries. But the owners mostly sell bread, which they bake fresh every day. Inside the glass counter is a tumble of fresh rolls, and the shelves are stacked with warm loaves of white bread. The smell of all this fresh bread is so good that Patita is hungry again, even after *Tia* (Aunt) Mercedes' pie. Sometimes her mother gives her a little extra money so she can choose a cookie or small pastry to eat as she walks or rides home.

Patita hops on her bike for a quick trip to the bakery. ▶

Patita debates with herself over which treat she should choose for a snack.

Dinner with Patita's Family

Anna Losada is an accountant for a German-Peruvian firm that owns many businesses in Peru. She works until 2:00 p.m. and rides home on the bus before Patita is home from school. Soon after, Patita and her mother begin dinner, cooking everything from fresh ingredients. Prepared foods are available in Peru, but they are not very popular. Many people in Peru have little storage space and no refrigerator or freezer to keep prepared foods. Plus, with markets everywhere, they are used to buying fresh ingredients.

Each meal begins with a salad, either of fresh greens or cooked vegetables, such as potato salad. Sometimes they have a homemade soup before the main course of beef, chicken, or fish. They have rice at most meals, but sometimes they eat spaghetti instead. Patita's favorite foods are chicken and rice or the Chinese dishes her mother sometimes prepares for their family.

The cobs of Peruvian corn are so thick that Mrs. Losada has to hit the back of the knife with a rock to cut them.

Patita's cousins Norma and Carlita often eat at their grandmother's house.

Inset: Patita likes all the different ways her mother cooks chicken and rice.

Corn on the cob is a popular vegetable in Peru, but both the ears of corn and the kernels are much bigger than corn in North America. Anna Losada chops ears of corn into serving-sized pieces before she boils them.

Aji de Gallina is a traditional Peruvian chicken dish. Most people use many hot peppers in the sauce, but Patita's family doesn't like very spicy foods, so Anna Losada leaves out some of the peppers. Patita likes it best the way her mother cooks it.

The Losadas' big kitchen table always seems crowded. Only on holidays and birthdays do they eat in the dining room since everyone feels more at home in the kitchen.

Patita doesn't cook meals by herself but helps her mother by washing and cutting up vegetables and setting the table. It's also her job to bring food from the stove to the table. Sometimes the steaming food looks so good that she cannot resist sampling a little bite on the way. She's glad that a five-foot (1.5-m) tall wall separates the cooking part of the kitchen from the table!

Everyone gathers at the table to eat meals together. Unless Patita stays at her aunt's to have dinner with Carlita, she and her family always have meals together. Everyone tells about their day at dinner; laughter and talk fill the air.

"I think the rice is ready," Patita tells her mother as she stirs the pot.

Patita and her cousin mix big pitchers of lemonade while their grandmother chops vegetables.

Markets in Peru

A supermarket stands only three blocks from their home, but Patita's mother would rather do her weekly shopping on Saturday morning at an open market. Here, farm families, called *campesinos*, gather on weekends to sell the fruit, vegetables, and meat they have raised on their farms. Many people in the city agree with Anna Losada that the food in these markets is fresher and better than the food that has been shipped to the grocery stores on trucks and trains.

Along with these open markets and grocery stores are small neighborhood shops, like the bakery. On the main streets, sidewalk vendors sell fruit and small items that they carry in baskets or in little pushcarts.

Top: Potatoes were unknown in Europe until the Spanish brought them back from Peru.

Bottom: Many Indians carry produce to market in large baskets or tie it to their backs with shawls.

Shoppers in Lima welcome the fresh-picked fruits and vegetables sold in the street markets.

Many Indians who are skilled in handicrafts such as weaving, pottery, knitting, basket making, or embroidery also sell their crafts in open markets or on the streets. Not far from Patita's house is an area where a number of these artisans have little booths. She can also visit a craft market in one park any evening.

Cooking Potatoes — Peruvian Style

Of all the fruits and vegetables found in the markets of Peru, the most common is the potato, with hundreds of varieties in all sizes and colors. There is even one kind that the Indians in the mountains dry for winter use. In the days of the Incas, these dried potatoes were stored in caves to feed the pople when the crops were poor.

The best-known Peruvian potato dish is *Papas a la Huancaina* (PAH-pas ah lah hoo-ahn-ky-EEN-ah), one of Patita's favorites. You can make them, too. Since you will need to cook them on a hot stove, you should ask an adult to help you. You will need:

8 small potatoes
2 cups (500 ml) of coarsely grated or chopped Muenster cheese
4 teaspoons (20 ml) of turmeric
A pinch of cayenne pepper
3/4 cup (187.5 ml) of heavy cream
1/3 cup (82.5 ml) of olive oil
Lettuce leaves

Wash the potatoes and boil them with their skins on until they are tender. Drain them, and as soon as they are cool enough to handle, peel off their skins. Keep the potatoes warm.

In a blender, combine the cheese, turmeric, pepper, and cream. Blend until smooth. Heat the oil in a skillet, pour in the cheese mixture, and turn the heat to very low. Stirring constantly with a wooden spoon, cook until the sauce is thick and smooth. Line a plate with lettuce leaves, put the potatoes over them, and pour the sauce over the potatoes. Serve them hot.

Papas a la Huancaina are nutritious enough for a main dish. ▶

Relaxing on the Weekend

After a busy week, Saturday and Sunday are times for the family to relax together. In warm weather, they all spend at least one day each weekend at El Bosque, a nearby beach on the Pacific Ocean.

On weekends all through the year, Uncle Pedro takes Patita to the Circulo Italiano, a sports club. Here she can swim in the pool, play basketball or volleyball with her cousin Pedrito, or take aerobics lessons. After all that exercise, they are thirsty, so Uncle Pedro usually buys them an Orange Crush soda at the snack bar in the clubhouse.

When Patita's classmates have birthdays, they sometimes invite the whole class to their homes for parties on Saturday night. Many of these classmates live so far apart that they rarely see each other outside of school, so these birthday get-togethers are extra special. Everyone talks, eats pizza, and dances to music from the radio.

As Patita gets older, she hopes to do more things with her friends. But she is glad that even when she is a grown-up, her life will still center on her home and her close-knit family.

The boys at a birthday party for Patita's friend are showing off again!

FOR YOUR INFORMATION: Peru

Official Name: República del Peru
(ray-POO-blee-kah del PAY-roo)
Republic of Peru

Capital: Lima

History

The First Inhabitants

People have lived in Peru for about 13,000 years. By about the year 1500 BC, they grew enough food crops so that all their time did not have to be spent hunting and gathering food. This gave them spare time for other activities, such as constructing buildings and decorating everyday items.

The earliest major ancient civilization in Peru, the Chavin culture in the north, was well established by 850 BC. The Chavin built the first South American religious structure and the first known three-story building, complete with rooms, galleries, stairs, and even ventilation.

Villages such as this one near Cuzco are often very poor, so many men go to Lima to try to find work.

The next period of development was from about 300 BC until around AD 500. The greatest cultures of this time were the Paracas, the Moche, and the Nazca.

By about 100 BC, the Paracas were building their own civilization a few hundred miles to the south in a narrow, dry strip of land between the Pacific Ocean and the Andes Mountains. The dry climate of the area has preserved both the burial shrouds and the bodies of the Paracas in their burial sites. From these, we've learned that the Paracas were expert weavers, producing some of the finest fabrics made by any early people. They used plant dyes to turn cotton and alpaca wool into brightly colored cloth with geometric borders and patterns of demons, people, and animals engaged in every sort of activity.

The Moche culture developed in the north after the decline of the Chavin, from about AD 100 to AD 600. Moche artisans made beautiful pottery showing scenes of daily life. Their leaders wore clothing decorated with gold, turquoise, coral, and shell. The men wore rings and necklaces and painted their legs to look like boots.

Lines in the Desert

No one knows what caused the end of the Paracas culture, but it disappeared, and in about AD 200, the Nazca civilization grew up in the same area. Like the Paracas, the Nazca did not leave great ruins of cities or religious temples. Instead, they left enormous outlines both of geometric designs and of pictures of animals and objects in the desert and on the hillsides. Since the Nazca had no written language, no record tells us what these etchings, known as Nazca lines, meant. Some historians have suggested that they were an attempt to talk with their gods, others that they were an astronomical means of calculating the seasons. Some people have even suggested that the lines were a way to communicate with creatures from outer space!

The Moche, Paracas, Nazca, and lesser known tribes were followed by more highly developed cultures such as the Tiahuanaco in the mountain highlands and the Chimu on Peru's northern coast.

The Aymara people founded the Tiahuanaco civilization. Strong and well organized, the Aymara dominated the tribes around them from about AD 600 until about AD 1000, when the culture disintegrated. The center of their culture, near Lake Titicaca, was an impressive place with a gateway carved from a single block of stone.

The Chimu peoples built their culture along the north coast and, by the year 1100, had an empire with a 600-mile (960-km) coastline. Best known as builders of the earliest planned walled cities in the Americas, the Chimu constructed cities with streets, reservoirs, and storehouses, as well as different types of housing for the people and their leaders. Some of the irrigation projects they built are still used today.

The Climax of Native Culture: The Inca

Around the beginning of the 13th century, a people arose near Lake Titicaca who rapidly overcame all other native peoples and formed one of the world's greatest empires. Today, they are best known by the name they used for each of their rulers — Inca. By the 15th century, they controlled all of the lands from the Andes to the Pacific Ocean and from what is now Colombia as far south as Santiago, Chile, including parts of Argentina.

The Inca were highly organized and changed each conquered tribe to suit their needs. For example, they retrained the sons of conquered leaders to do things the Inca way and then returned them as the leaders of the area near their homes. The Inca used irrigation and terraced the slopes of high Andes ridges to improve their farming. They stored crops in large buildings to provide food in times of drought. Although they did not use the wheel for transportation, they built roads connecting all of their cities. An organized system of relay runners provided rapid communication throughout their empire.

Although they had no written language, the Inca created a special spoken language that they taught throughout their empire so that all of their people would understand one another. Quechua, which is spoken today throughout the former Inca lands, is derived from that language.

The Conquest by Spain: A New Empire Rises

In 1532, a Spanish soldier named Francisco Pizarro set out to conquer this huge empire. With 183 men and 37 horses, he landed on the coast of Peru. Hearing that the Inca king, Atahualpa, was inland, he went over the high mountains to find him. When Atahualpa tried to be friendly with the Spanish, they tricked him, killing his guards and holding him for ransom. Even though his subjects brought huge amounts of gold to pay the ransom, enough to fill a large room, Atahualpa was killed.

The Inca that followed Atahualpa tried to fight on. But while the Spanish had guns, cannon, horses, steel swords, and metal armor, the Inca had only slings, spears, and arrows. The Spanish also brought new diseases to the continent, and the Indians died from these and from the poor treatment that they received.

Within 40 years, the government of the Inca disappeared, and the Spanish controlled their subjects, who are now called Indians. The Spanish moved away or killed the Indian leaders and compelled the people to mine gold and silver that was melted down into bars and sent to the King of Spain. The Indians were also forced to give up their religion, accept the Catholic faith, and pay heavy taxes to officials and to the church. The impoverished Indians' land was divided among the Spanish conquerors and deeded to nobles back in Spain. Within 300 years of the arrival of the Spanish, the population of Indians dropped from 15 million to three million.

Independence Comes to Peru

Spain was a cruel and greedy master, and the people in South America grew tired of having all the wealth of their lands sent overseas. In 1810, Simón Bolívar started the war for the liberation of Venezuela, and in 1816, José de San Martín began the revolution that freed Argentina. By 1821, Argentina was independent, and San Martín went to Peru to write the Peruvian Declaration of Independence. In 1823, the liberator of Venezuela, Bolívar, was invited to Peru to help drive out the Spanish. By the end of the decade, Peru and all of South America was independent.

But independence did not bring democracy, and it did nothing to make the lives of the Indians better. All of the money and power in the country remained in the hands of a very few people who owned most of the good land. Large foreign companies were set up to mine the copper, zinc, lead, silver, and gold. They hired Indian workers but paid them very little.

Dictators and Debt

After independence, Peru was run by a series of military and nonmilitary dictators. An early attempt to create a federation with Chile, Peru, and Bolivia was defeated. In 1845, Ramón Castilla, a *mestizo* (that is, a person of mixed Spanish and Indian blood), became president. His government built schools as well as railroads and telegraph lines that drew distant parts of the country together. He also reduced some of the taxes on the Indians. With a break of only four years, he ruled from 1845 until 1862.

Despite these improvements, Peru was troubled by debt. For example, although Peru defeated Spain's attempt to regain its lost colonies in 1865, the war cost the country dearly. In addition, Castilla's successor decided to build a railroad over the mountains, and the tremendous cost of the project put Peru even further in debt.

The Atacama Desert in the southern part of Peru was rich with deposits of nitrate, a chemical that is used to make fertilizer and explosives. In the 1880s, Chile tried to take over this desert. Peru and its ally Bolivia fought against this attempt in the War of the Pacific, a disaster for Peru. Many people were killed, the navy was sunk, and almost all factories within firing distance of the coast were destroyed. By the end of the war, Peru owed so much money to foreign countries that nearly all her trade and commerce belonged to foreigners.

By the time of World War I in 1914, there was a small wealthy class, but the Indians had no land, no money, and no way to adequately feed and clothe themselves. In 1924, a student named Víctor Haya de la Torre started a political party called the American Popular Revolutionary Alliance (APRA). Its purpose was to reduce the power of the military and to improve the welfare of all Peruvians, including the Indians. While the government during this century has been dominated by a small group of wealthy people, the popularity of APRA has led to the government's adoption of some of APRA's programs. Education for all children was made compulsory, and the working hours of men, women, and children became more humane.

In 1968, the army overthrew the elected government and installed a military government with a general as president and other military officers as his cabinet. Another coup replaced that government in 1975. The military spent large amounts of money on weapons and on huge projects, using money borrowed from European countries and the United States. It wasn't until 1980 that a president was chosen in a free election. In 1990, Alberto Fujimori was elected president, and his first problem was to find solutions to the huge debt caused by the years of military rule.

Peru's Problems

In recent years, the economy of Peru has been very bad. Many Indians and mestizos who used to live in the rural areas have moved to Lima and other cities to look — usually unsuccessfully — for work. The government has been unable to provide for their care. Many try to make money by selling soap, food, and other small items along the streets. Without an income, many have had to live in shacks of cardboard and tin built in vacant lots. Because of the poor and unsanitary living conditions, diseases spread quickly. In 1991, a cholera epidemic struck thousands of Peruvians.

In the past few years, another serious problem has hurt Peru. Two rebel groups, the Shining Path and the Tupac Amaru, have attacked embassies in Lima, as well as trains, buses, stores, and entire villages. These attacks have killed and hurt many innocent people and left others fearing for their lives. They have also frightened away tourists who would bring in badly needed foreign money and companies considering investing in Peruvian businesses.

Government

Peru has had many constitutions since its independence. The 1980 constitution allows for free elections and permits political parties. Although the wealthy still control politics, socialists strongly influence politics, as do small but often violent communist groups.

The legislative branch of government, called the Congress, has a Senate of 60 members and a Chamber of Deputies with 180 members. Elected every five years, the members are responsible for making the laws.

The president and a council of ministers appointed by him are responsible for running the government and carrying out the laws. The president and the council are also responsible for the daily operation of all government agencies. The president is elected for a term of five years. All citizens of Peru over 18 years old are eligible to vote and are required to cast a ballot in each election. Voters are not required to be able to read and write. Women have been able to vote since 1955.

There are several different levels of courts. Most minor criminal cases and those involving small amounts of money are tried in front of a justice of the peace. More serious criminal cases and those involving more money are tried before judges in the provincial capitals. The top judicial level where cases are appealed is called the Supreme Court.

Currency

The Peruvian unit of currency is called the *Inti*. Inflation has been so severe in Peru that the Inti is now worth very little. In December 1991, a new unit of currency, the New *Sol* (Sun) was established, with each New Sol equal to one million Intis. All of the currency is paper since Inti coins would not be very practical.

One million Intis are equal to one New Sol, which has about the same value as one dollar in US money.

Peoples and Languages

Peru has a population of about 22,332,000, which consists primarily of three different groups. The largest group is of pure Indian ancestry and forms about 46% of Peru's population. Of the several different groups of Indians within this large group, the three main ones are the Quechua, the Aymara, and the Campa. All three were once part of the people ruled by the Inca.

The Quechua are the peoples of the Andes highlands and the coastal areas. They all speak the old official Inca language, Quechua, and make up the single largest group of Indians in Peru. The second largest group of Indians, the Aymara, lives primarily in the high Andean area near the shore of Lake Titicaca along the Peru-Bolivia border. Some even live on floating islands in the lake! The smallest of the three principal Indian groups in Peru, the Campa, lives in the part of the Andes where the high mountain peaks descend into the rain forests and swamps that drain into the Amazon River. The Campa are hunters and live an isolated and primitive life.

After the Indians, the next largest group is called *mestizo*, which is the Spanish word for people of mixed Indian and Spanish parentage. The mestizos make up about 38% of the population. They usually speak Spanish and think of themselves as Spanish.

Only about 15% of the population is of European, usually Spanish, ancestry, unmixed with any Indian blood. Although they make up a smaller percentage of the population than the mestizos or Indians, the Spanish in Peru tend to be wealthier and are in the higher levels of government and business than the other two groups. Peru also has a small percentage of people of Asian and African origin.

Both Spanish and Quechua are the official languages of Peru. About 68% of all Peruvians speak Spanish and 27% speak Quechua. Another 3% speak Aymara. Although many people can speak more than one of these languages, a large number of people can only speak the Indian language spoken by their families.

Traditional Arts, Crafts, and Music

Peru's arts show the influence of its Indian heritage. Pottery, weaving, woodcarving, leather work, and silver and gold work are all popular crafts now, as they were in pre-Spanish conquest times. Even the designs used today are based on the traditional ones of the Inca.

Pottery and ceramic work, which began long before the Inca, are perhaps the best known crafts outside Peru today. Ceramic beads with tiny designs of llamas and local scenes are found in Peruvian jewelry that is popular throughout the world. In many rural areas, especially in the Andes, weavers provide much of the income for families. In the markets of Cuzco or even on the trails between mountain villages, you often see women spinning wool on drop spindles almost exactly like the ones used centuries ago.

Like its crafts, the music of Peru also shows its Indian origins. Reed pipes from the mountain country, combined with stringed, guitarlike instruments and wooden drums, provide the music that is popular in the villages. In the parks of Lima, groups of street musicians play traditional songs of the Andes.

Land and Climate

Peru is in the northwest part of the South American continent. The Pacific Ocean forms the western border of the country; Ecuador and Colombia are to the north, Brazil and Bolivia to the east, and Chile to the south.

A narrow strip of land that is extremely dry and desertlike runs along the Pacific coast. Immediately east of this coastal area, the land rises suddenly to form the Andes Mountains. These mountains occupy almost the entire western half of Peru. Scattered throughout the Andes are grassy highland plains. In the east, the mountains descend through a series of foothills to a highland plain. The largest part of this plain is in the Amazon rain forest.

The highest peaks in the Andes are from 18,000 to 22,000 feet (5,490 m to 6,710 m). The slopes are very steep and are cut through in many places by ravines and canyons, some more than twice as deep as the Grand Canyon. These mountains have always been a barrier to communication and transportation and are the main reason Peru's interior is so undeveloped. Roads and railroads to move goods and people are difficult and costly to build and maintain; travel on them is slow because of the many curved and winding roads, or switchbacks, needed to climb the mountains.

The climate along the coast is generally hot and dry. The average rainfall in Lima is less than two inches (5 cm) a year, but for many years in a row, there may be no rain at all. Inland, warmer air containing moisture that evaporates from the Pacific Ocean collides with the mountains, and rainfall is greater there. The height of the mountains also prevents cooler air from passing, so the area east of the Andes is tropical. The highest parts of the mountains are very cold and snowy, and some places have permanent snow cover.

PERU – Political and Physical

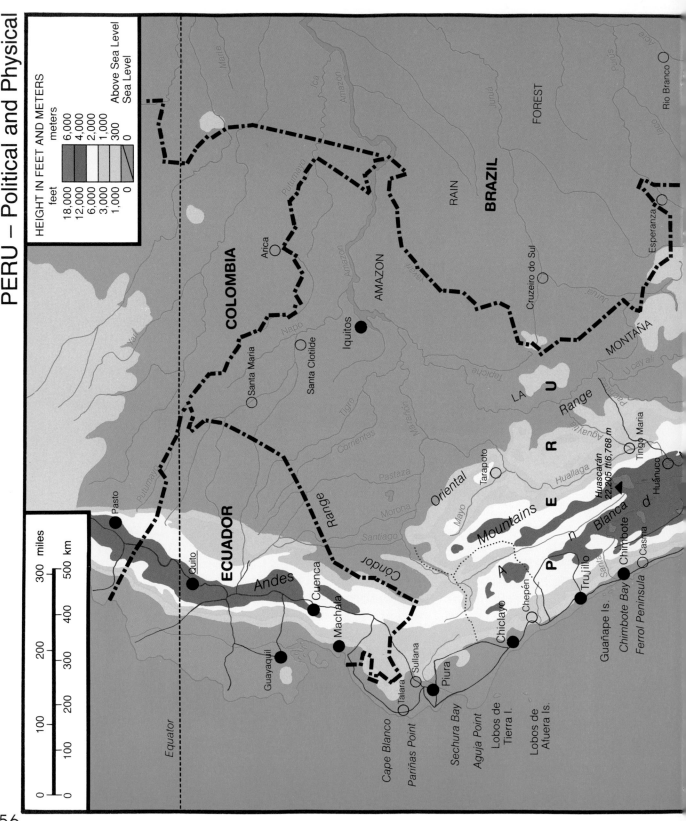

HEIGHT IN FEET AND METERS

feet	meters
18,000	6,000
12,000	4,000
6,000	2,000
3,000	1,000
1,000	300
0	0

Above Sea Level

Sea Level

300 miles
500 km

0   100   200   300   400   500 km
0   100   200   300 miles

Equator

COLOMBIA

ECUADOR

BRAZIL

Pasto

Quito

Cuenca

Machala

Guayaquil

Talara

Sullana

Piura

Cape Blanco

Pariñas Point

Sechura Bay

Aguja Point

Lobos de Tierra I.

Lobos de Afuera Is.

Chiclayo

Chepén

Trujillo

Guañape Is.

Chimbote

Chimbote Bay

Ferrol Peninsula

Casma

Huánuco

Tingo Maria

Huascarán
22,205 ft/6,768 m

Blanca

Cordillera

Andes

Condor Range

Oriental Range

Mountains

Tarapoto

LA MONTAÑA

P E R U

RAIN FOREST

AMAZON

Iquitos

Santa Clotilde

Santa Maria

Arica

Cruzeiro do Sul

Rio Branco

Esperanza

Pastaza

Morona

Santiago

Marañón

Tigre

Corrientes

Napo

Putumayo

Amazon

Amazon

Ica

Maria

Yari

Juruá

Purus

Acre

Huallaga

Mayo

Ucayali

Tapiche

56

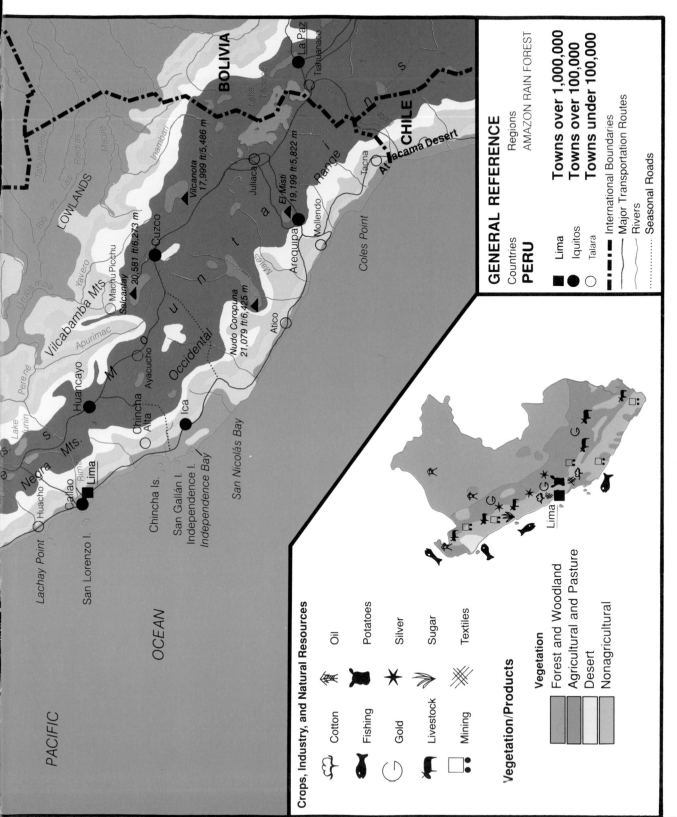

GENERAL REFERENCE

Countries   Regions
PERU   AMAZON RAIN FOREST

■ Lima   **Towns over 1,000,000**
● Iquitos   **Towns over 100,000**
○ Talara   **Towns under 100,000**

▬·▬·▬ International Boundaries
——— Major Transportation Routes
〜〜〜 Rivers
··········· Seasonal Roads

Crops, Industry, and Natural Resources

Cotton   Oil

Fishing   Potatoes

Gold   Silver

Livestock   Sugar

Mining   Textiles

Vegetation/Products

Vegetation

Forest and Woodland

Agricultural and Pasture

Desert

Nonagricultural

Map labels

PACIFIC OCEAN

BOLIVIA

CHILE

La Paz
Tiahuanaco
Lake Titicaca
Juliaca
Vilcanota 17,999 ft/5,486 m ▲
El Misti 19,199 ft/5,822 m ▲
Arequipa
Mollendo
Tacna
Atacama Desert
Coles Point

Cuzco
Salcantay 20,581 ft/6,273 m ▲
Machu Picchu
Nudo Coropuna 21,079 ft/6,425 m ▲
Atico
Ica
Chincha Alta
Ayacucho
Huancayo
Vilcabamba Mts.
Occidental
Andes Mts.
Negra Mts.
Lima
Callao
Huacho
Lachay Point
San Lorenzo I.
Chincha Is.
San Gallán I.
Independence I.
Independence Bay
San Nicolás Bay

LOWLANDS

Rio de las Piedras
Tahuamanu
Madre
Heath
Inambari
Yavero
Apurimac
Urubamba
Perené
Lake Junin
Rimac
Malas

57

Agriculture, Industry, and Natural Resources

The political and economic heart of Peru lies in the narrow band of land along the Pacific Ocean. Most of the manufacturing and trade is centered there; factories produce textiles, cement, steel, televisions, processed food, tires, and chemical and petrochemical products. Although most of this coastal land is a desert, there is enough irrigation in some fertile areas to grow crops. Farming communities grow corn, cotton, sugar cane, and rice.

Much of the land in the Andes highlands is good for raising food crops and livestock on small farms or on large *haciendas*, or ranching farms. Although some of the Inca's steep mountain terraces are still used by the Indians, most food is now grown on the fertile river valley floors between the high peaks. In the mountains, the main crops are potatoes, corn, wheat, and barley. In fact, these mountains are the original source of corn and potatoes. Over 400 different kinds of potato are grown in the highlands, including one kind that the Indians have dried for winter use ever since the time of the Inca. The mountains also hold most of the mineral wealth of the country. Besides the gold that brought the Spanish, silver, copper, mercury, vanadium, and coal are mined. Some oil and natural gas have also been found in Peru.

Sheep, llamas, and alpacas provide wool for knitting and weaving. Fish, shellfish, and fishmeal are sold in the country and exported as well. But during the cholera epidemic in 1991, Peru's fishing industry was almost destroyed as countries banned its import because of a fear of contaminated fish.

Religion

Nearly 90% of Peruvians are Catholics, but many of these are Indians who combine the beliefs of the Catholic faith with the customs and traditions of their native faiths. The saints' days of Catholicism are often blended with ancient seasonal festivals based on harvesting or planting. Many Indian Christians also worship Inca gods. The other 10% of the population follow Bahai or various Asian or other imported religions or follow no organized religion.

Education

All children between the ages of seven and sixteen are required to attend elementary school, and these schools are free. Secondary education (high school level) is also free, but students are not required to attend. The schools vary greatly in the quality of education; some parents give up a lot so that their children can attend a private school, where the chance of being able to attend college after graduation is much higher. Almost a half million students attend Peru's 35 universities.

Sports and Recreation

Soccer, called *fútbol* (football), is the national sport. Schools and sports clubs have their own teams, and boys play street soccer with whatever ball is available. Lima's National Stadium is decorated with painted laurel wreaths showing the names of Peru's best-loved athletes. Peruvians honor their female atheletes; about half of the sports stars named are women.

Lima

A city of nearly six million people, Lima is located on Peru's coast. It was Peru's original capital, founded in 1535 by the Spanish conquerors. Now a modern city, it retains the churches and fine mansions from its earliest days. These are in the ornate Spanish architectural style, with delicate, carved wooden balconies overlooking the streets. In past centuries, it was considered improper for ladies to be seen by people passing on the street, so wooden screens were carved to hide them when they sat outdoors in the afternoon.

Lima has many wide avenues. In the center of the old city stands the Plaza de Las Armas, which is a large square surrounded by the Cathedral, the President's Palace, and other public buildings.

The cathedral in Lima is one of the largest in South America.

Peruvians in North America

There are no large concentrations of immigrants from Peru in North America, but there has been a recent wave of immigration of an unusual kind. North American families are adopting Peruvian babies orphaned by poverty, disease, or terrorist attacks on their families. Nearly every airline flight between Lima and the United States carries several Peruvian infants moving north to begin a new life with their adoptive parents.

Glossary of Important Terms

cholera .... an often fatal infectious disease caused by bacteria in food or water.

drop spindle .... a stick around which thread is wound as the thread is made by twisting the fibers by hand.

fishmeal .... a mealy substance made from fish parts and used as fertilizer and animal feed.

mestizo .... a person of European and American Indian background.

switchback .... a road or trail that goes up a steep slope in a winding path.

vanadium .... a soft, bright white metal. When combined with other metals, it's used to make engine parts, as a developing agent in photography, and as a drying agent in paints.

Glossary of Useful Spanish Terms

adios (ah-dee-OHS) .... goodbye

bien (BYEN) .... well (as in "I am fine")

Como esta Usted? (KOH-moh STAH oo-STED) .... How are you?

De nada (day NAH-dah) .... You are welcome

gracias (GRAH-see-uhs) .... thank you

ola (OH-lah) .... hello

por favor (por fah-VOR) .... please

si (SEE) .... yes

Glossary of Useful Quechua Terms

ama jina kaychu (AH-mah JEE-nah
    KAY-choo) ....please
taitacha pagasunki (tay-TAH-chah
    pah-gah-SOON-kee) ....thank you
ari (ah-REE)...yes
mana (MAH-nah) ....no
mama (MAH-mah) ....mother
taita (TYE-tah) ....father

More Books about Peru

A Family in Peru. St. John (Lerner Publications)
Mystery in Peru: The Lines of Nazca. Lye (Franklin Watts)
Peru. (Chelsea House)
Peru in Pictures. Staff (Lerner Publications)

Things To Do — Research Projects and Activities

In recent years, coca leaf production, which is refined into the illegal drug cocaine, has become a major industry in Peru. Peru's government is trying to eliminate the drug traffic and to find new cash crops for farmers.

As you read about Peru and its struggle to improve the lives of its people, be aware of the importance of having current information. Some of the activities and projects below require up-to-date information. Two publications your library may have will tell you about recent magazine and newspaper articles on Peru and other topics:

Readers' Guide to Periodical Literature
Children's Magazine Guide

1. Rebel groups calling themselves the Shining Path and Tupac Amaru use terrorist methods to disrupt the government and economy of Peru. Find out if they have been active lately. What do these people hope to accomplish? What methods do they use? Are they successful? What is the government doing to try to stop them? Write a report on these terrorist groups.

2. Peru has a long coastline along the Pacific Ocean. How does that affect the country's business and trade? Does it have a history as a seafaring

nation? Is fishing or any other ocean activity important to Peru's economy? Write a report on the importance of the sea to Peru.

3. If you could meet Patita in person, what questions would you ask her about Peru, her school, or her family? What would you tell her about your own school or family?

4. Peru celebrates many holidays that are similar to those in North America. For example, Halloween has its origins in the same church holiday as the Peruvian Day of the Dead. What other festivals do we share? How are these alike and how do they differ? Find an activity or make a decoration from a Peruvian holiday that you can enjoy on a similar holiday here.

5. If you would like a pen pal in Peru, write to:

International Pen Friends
P.O. Box 290065
Brooklyn, NY 11229

Worldwide Pen Friends
P.O. Box 39097
Downey, CA 90241

Be sure to tell them what country you want your pen pal to be from and include your full name, age, and address.

Index

Machu Picchu 30, 32
markets 38, 42, 44
mental retardation 16
military 51, 52
mining 51, 52, 58
music 55

names 6
natural resources 58
Nazca lines 49
New *Sol* 53
nitrates 52
North America 60

Pacific Ocean 46, 49, 50, 55, 58
parks 8
PEOPLES 54; African 54; Asian 54;
    Aymara 49, 54; Campa 54;
    Chavin 48, 49; Chimu 49-50;
    European 54; Inca 29, 30, 31,
    34, 54, 58; Indian 10, 29, 42,
    43, 44, 51, 52, 54; *mestizos* 52,
    54; Moche 49; Nazca 49;
    Paracas 49; Quechua 54;
    Spanish 29, 42, 50-51, 54, 58
Pizarro, Francisco 50
plants 10, 24
politics 52, 53
president 52, 53
pueblos jovenes 10

recreation 17, 46, 59
RELIGIONS 51, 58; Bahai 58;
    Catholicism 20, 29, 51, 58; Inca
    29, 58; Methodist 20
religious structures 30, 48

San Martín, José de 51
Santiago 50
Senate 53
sheep 58

Shining Path 53
socialists 53
South America 6, 34, 51, 55
Spain 51
Spanish conquest 29, 50-51, 59
sports 12, 46, 59
Supreme Court 53

taxes 51
terrorism 53, 60
Tiahuanaco 49
transportation 50, 55
Tupac Amaru 53
typewriters 25

United States 52, 60

Venezuela 51

War of the Pacific 52
weapons 50-51, 52
World War I 52